The Wind in the Willows

Kenneth Grahame

TEACHER GUIDE

NOTE:

The trade book edition of the novel used to prepare this guide is found in the Novel Units catalog and on the Novel Units website. Using other editions may have varied page references.

Please note: We have assigned Interest Levels based on our knowledge of the themes and ideas of the books included in the Novel Units sets, however, please assess the appropriateness of this novel or trade book for the age level and maturity of your students prior to reading with them. You know your students best!

ISBN 978-1-56137-208-9

Copyright infringement is a violation of Federal Law.

© 2020 by Novel Units, Inc., St. Louis, MO. All rights reserved. No part of this publication may be reproduced, translated, stored in a retrieval system, or transmitted in any way or by any means (electronic, mechanical, photocopying, recording, or otherwise) without prior written permission from Novel Units, Inc.

Reproduction of any part of this publication for an entire school or for a school system, by for-profit institutions and tutoring centers, or for commercial sale is strictly prohibited.

Novel Units is a registered trademark of Conn Education.

Printed in the United States of America.

To order, contact your local school supply store, or:

Toll-Free Fax: 877.716.7272
Phone: 888.650.4224
3901 Union Blvd., Suite 155
St. Louis, MO 63115

sales@novelunits.com

novelunits.com

Table of Contents

Summary 3

Initiating Activities 4

Bulletin Board Ideas 6

Vocabulary Activities 6

Author's Craft 8

Twelve Chapters 17
    Chapters contain: Vocabulary,
    Discussion Questions, and
    Supplementary Activities

Culminating Activities 33

Post-reading Extension Activities 34

Assessment 35

Skills and Strategies

Thinking
Brainstorming, classifying and categorizing, evaluating, analyzing details

Writing
Descriptive, figurative language, persuasive

Literary Elements
Character, setting, plot, conflict, figurative language, fantasy

Comprehension
Predicting, sequencing, cause/effect, propaganda, fantasy and realism, comparison/contrast, inference

Vocabulary
Prefixes/suffixes, root words

Listening/Speaking
Discussions, role-play

Summary

Mole, disgusted with spring cleaning, sets out to see what is going on in the world around him. He meets Water Rat, with whom he goes on a boat ride, has a picnic, and becomes friends. Rat introduces Mole to Toad in Toad's grand home, and then the three set out on an adventure in one of Toad's newest fascinations—a gypsy cart. Disaster strikes when a man in a motor-car scares the horse, causing the cart to be wrecked. However, as a result, Toad becomes enamored with his newest craze—a motor-car.

By winter time, Mole has become impatient to meet Badger and proceeds to enter the Wild Wood in search of him. Mole gets lost in a snowstorm. Rat finds him, and together they chance upon Badger's home, where they are welcomed, warmed, and fed by the reclusive Mr. Badger. Mole and Badger become friends as they find they share common ideas of "home," and Badger gives Mole a tour of his home. As Mole and Rat make their way back to the river, Mole is drawn to his former home. The resourceful Rat puts together a feast for himself, Mole, and the Yuletide carolers who arrive. After spending the night, they return to the river.

In early summer, Mr. Badger, Mole, and Rat go on a mission of mercy to rescue Toad from himself and his latest and most powerful motor-car. They accost Toad, strip him of his riding gear, lecture him on his folly, lock him in his room, and attempt to guard him. Ingenious Mr. Toad escapes, steals a motor-car, and is eventually arrested and imprisoned.

Rat and Mole set out to find Little Portly, the Otter's missing son. While rowing, they are drawn to an island in the river from which they hear beautiful music emanating. There they see Pan, the country-god, playing his flute while standing watch over Little Portly. Little Portly is rescued, but, as decreed, Mole and Rat become instantly oblivious to the wondrous scene they have witnessed.

While stagnating in prison, the gaoler's daughter befriends Toad and helps him escape as a washerwoman. Realizing he has no money to buy a ticket, Toad begs a ride from the engine-driver of a local train. The police realize what he has done and give chase, but Toad escapes into the woods. Back at the river, fall has come, and one by one the animals are departing southward or preparing for winter, leaving Rat despondent. Along comes a seafaring rat, enthralling Rat with tales of his travels. In a dreamlike state, Rat packs and sets out to live the seafaring life, but Mole compels him to stay home. Patient Mole gradually revives Rat from the depths of depression with accountings of local happenings and lures him to begin writing poetry again.

Toad makes his way to a nearby canal where he is offered a ride by a barge-woman. His false identity revealed, he is thrown from the barge. He seeks revenge by stealing the barge-woman's horse and selling it to a gypsy. Nearing home, he chances upon the same motor-car which he had stolen earlier. Still in his disguise, he finagles a ride and an opportunity to drive the car again. After crashing the car and being nearly caught by the police, he falls into the river and is carried along by the current until he manages to pull himself out at the door to Rat's hole.

During Toad's absence, his home has been taken over by stoats, weasels, and ferrets. Badger and Mole develop a plan by which the four friends could retake Toad Hall by entering the house through a secret passage. They quickly rout the weasels, ferrets, and stoats in a surprise attack. Then they invite their friends to a celebration banquet.

At last, all is nearly returned to normal. The four heroes are lauded by the river folk and those of the Wild Wood. A reformed Toad duly thanks and properly compensates the gaoler's daughter, the engine-driver, and the barge-woman (the last, against his will).

Initiating Activities

1. Prediction: Have students examine the cover illustration and title, then flip through the book. Ask: What kind of book do you suppose this will be? What is suggested by the title? Ask students to determine the four animals present and the setting. What evidence is there that would lead you to believe that this is a book of fiction or non-fiction, or of fantasy or realistic fiction?

2. Reviews and Summary: Read aloud the remark on the back cover and the back-cover summary. Ask: What does the back-cover summary tell you about what to expect from this book?

3. Have students read about the life of Kenneth Grahame. Have them list 10-15 important events in his life. Research and tell the students how *The Wind in the Willows* came to be written.

4. Prereading Discussion Topics: Encourage free, open-ended discussion on these topics, or use them as writing assignments.

    Friends: What are some characteristics of people you consider to be your closest friends? What does it take to be a good friend to someone? Should friends always be honest with one another?

    Getting Back to Nature: Would you rather live in the city or the country? Do you like looking at plants and animals? How often do you "get back to nature"? What are the good things about spending time in the country? Do you think people who live in the country tend to have a different attitude toward wildlife than city-dwellers?

    Facing a Frightening Situation: What makes you afraid? Heights? The dark? Diving in deep water? Electrical storms? What do you think about when you are afraid? How do you overcome your fear? Do animals become afraid? What do you think they fear?

5. Response Log: Have students keep a response log as they read. In one type of log, the students pretend to be one of the characters. Writing on one side of a piece of paper, the student writes in the first person about his or her reaction to what happened in the chapter. A partner responds to these writings on the other side of the paper, as if talking to the character.

In the dual-entry log, students jot down brief summaries and reactions to each section of the novel. (The first entry could be made based on a preview of the novel—a glance at the cover and a flip through the book.)

Pages	Summary	Reactions (Might begin...)
		"I liked the part when..."
		"This reminded me of the time I..."
		"If I were Toad..."

6. Geography: On a map of England, locate the Thames River, Cookham Dene in Berkshire, and Windsor Forest.

7. Language: Explain to the students that because of the time and the place that this book was written (England in the late 1800s), some of the spellings and sentence structures are different from the typical way we would spell or say them today. List the following examples from *The Wind in the Willows*:

Spellings: Colour, harbour, favour, faery, gaoler, recognisable

Sentence Structures: "Well, that's as may be" (page 180).
"And all because you must needs to go and steal a motor car" (page 202).
"...sit down to your supper along of us" (page 232)

Explain that our language is constantly evolving and that new words are being coined all the time. Discuss examples of differences in slang today, five years ago, ten years ago, etc. Develop a semantic map of new words that have come into the English language recently. Ask the children to note in their reading journals different spellings and unusual ways of saying things. For example: endeavoured (page 84), rancour (page 95), touzled (page 212).

8. Many stories have the same parts: a setting, a problem, a goal, and a series of events that lead to an ending or conclusion. These story elements can be placed on a story map. Just as a road map helps a driver get from one place to another, a story map leads a reader from one point to another. After reading the first chapter, what information do you have?

- What is the setting?
- Who are the main characters?
- What is the problem?

There are many types of story maps. Use a class story map and then, for a concluding activity, ask students to make their own type of map. (See page 16 of this guide.)

© Novel Units, Inc.　　　　　　　　　　　　　　　　　　　　　　　　　　　All rights reserved

Bulletin Board Ideas

1. Develop a bulletin board with a map of England that shows the locations of Kenneth Grahame's boyhood home and London. Add pictures of the English countryside. One might label examples of heath, hedgerows, downs, common, dells, hummocks, and copses.

2. Develop an interactive bulletin board on which the students can add unusual spellings and sentence structures which they find in the book. Students should list the page number where the example was found and give modern-day versions of the example.

Vocabulary Activities

There are a great many challenging vocabulary words in the novel *The Wind in the Willows*. Do not take away from the charm of the book by making the vocabulary too burdensome for the students.

1. Using the vocabulary lists in this guide, pronounce selected words for a particular section of the book. Do not use every word. Have students fill out a chart like the one below. They should predict the definition based on the way the word sounds, read the word in context, discuss context clues with others in class, and jot down the dictionary definition that fits the way the word is used in the novel.

Word	Prediction	Dictionary Definition

2. Have students "map" selected words that fit into the following framework:

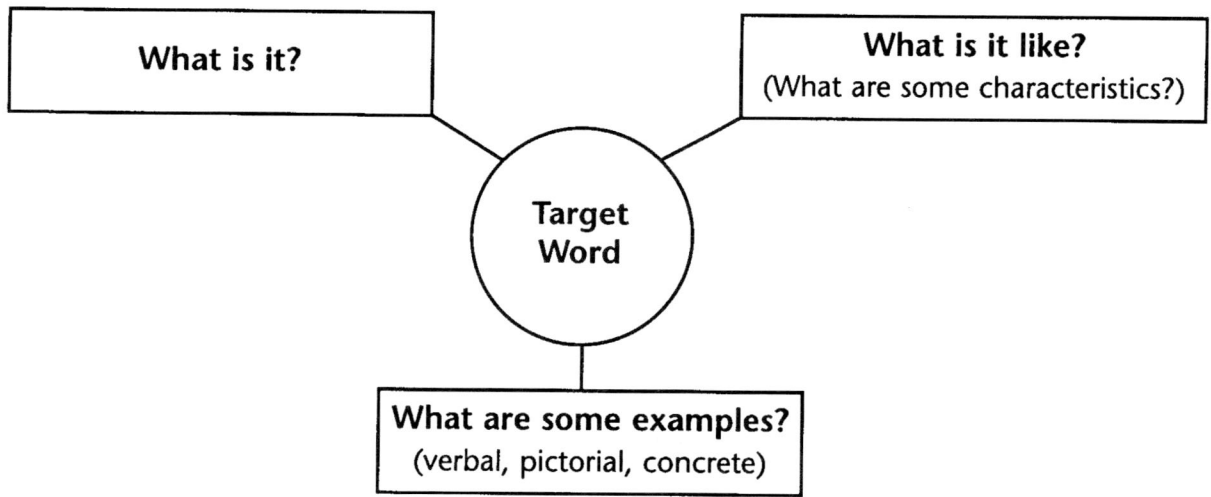

3. Have students choose two vocabulary words and explain how they go together.

4. Select vocabulary words that you consider important to know for the chapter. Ask students to alphabetize the selected words and define each of them, according to how it is used in the novel.

5. Have students select a group of words and use as many of them as possible in one sentence.

6. As a class, find the base or root word for at least eight vocabulary words. What is the meaning of the root word? What is the meaning of the vocabulary word? What prefixes and suffixes were added to the root word? How was the meaning of the root word changed by this addition?

7. Have the students act out some of the vocabulary words to find out if classmates can guess the target words. Some suggested words from *The Wind in the Willows* might include: row (page 2), togs (page 12), prostrate (page 15), dejected (page 16), revived (page 17), and bedraggled (page 17).

8. Have students sort vocabulary words into categories. Classify a group of words into names of things (nouns), action words (verbs), and describing words (adjectives and adverbs).

9. Have students use vocabulary words to play "Odd One Out." Select words from one or two chapters. Make a chain of four words, of which one is a vocabulary word and one does not belong. For example:
    Quest—Pursuit—Relinquish*—Search
    *"Relinquish" is not a synonym of "quest."

10. Challenge students to use as many of the words on the assigned list to write a letter to a character in the novel, or to a classmate. Some of the sentences in the letter can be a bit of a stretch, but should still make sense and demonstrate that the student understands the words' definitions.

11. Have students use graph paper or a software program to create crossword puzzles and clues for a specific list of words belonging to one or two reading sections. Have them trade their puzzles for solving.

12. Play a vocabulary challenge game. Use words from several chapters. The students work in pairs. One picks a word from the list, while another student asks three to five questions to discover the word and give the definition.

13. Upon completion of the novel, have students list the 20 vocabulary words they feel are most important to understanding the story. Have them write one sentence for each word, explaining why it is important for understanding *The Wind in the Willows*.

Author's Craft

Kenneth Grahame uses many techniques that capture the reader and make *The Wind in the Willows* a literary experience. As students read the novel, call attention to what the author is doing, and why.

Characterization

Characterization is the way an author informs the reader about what characters are like. Direct characterization is when the author describes the character. Indirect characterization is when the reader figures out what the character is like based on what he or she thinks, says, or does.

1. What words and phrases are used to describe Water Rat? *(Page 4, He has a grave brown face, a twinkle in his eye, small, neat ears, and thick, silky hair.)*
   This is direct characterization.

2. How do we know what kind of character Water Rat is? *(Pages 4-12, by how he talks to his friends, what he thinks about his neighbors, how he treats them, and how his neighbors act toward him)*
   This is indirect characterization.

As the story continues, students may find additional examples of characterization and add them to attribute webs. (See pages 13-15 of this guide.)

Conflict

Conflict is a struggle or problem that makes a story interesting. There are several types of conflict:

1. A person against another person
2. A person against nature or society
3. Inner conflict, in which a character struggles with his or her own feelings.

Ask students to find an example of each type of conflict in *The Wind in the Willows*.

Suspense

Explain that suspense is a story quality that produces tension in the reader. The reader grows curious about what will happen next. Suspense usually raises one or two types of questions in the reader's mind: What will the outcome be? and, When will the inevitable outcome happen?

Have students discuss how suspense develops in each section. *(The reader wants to know, first: Can Rat and Mole save Toad from himself and his addiction to motor-cars? and later: Will Toad outwit the jailers and escape?)* Explain that suspense often depends on uncertainty about which of two opposing forces will "win" and the desire to see one force defeat the other. Ask: How do you feel about Toad? Do you want him to continue in his willful self-destruction, or do you see him as a hero in a grand adventure?

Atmosphere or Mood

Explain that the atmosphere of a story is the overall mood, the dominant emotional tone of a literary work. Atmosphere is created by the handling of setting, character, and theme.

Atmosphere can be developed using adjectives, such as:

- Page 1: "Spring was moving in the air above and in the earth below and around him, penetrating even his dark and lowly little house with its spirit of divine discontent and longing."
- Page 6: "The Mole waggled his toes from sheer happiness, spread his chest with a sigh of full contentment, and leaned back blissfully into the soft cushions."
- Page 16: "So the dismal Mole, wet without and ashamed within, trotted about till he was fairly dry..."

Ask students how they would describe the atmosphere. How has Grahame developed this atmosphere? For example, what words convey a sense of Mole's discomfort?

You might put the following chart on the board as you elicit suggestions about how the author sets a menacing or a happy atmosphere.

Page	Phrases to Describe Setting	Phrases to Describe Characters	Tone

Climax

Explain that the climax of a story is the point at which the conflict reaches its highest intensity and the reader's emotional response is at its greatest point. Ask: What was the climax of this story? *(Page 198, Toad crashes the motor-car, is again chased by the police, and jumps into the river to swim home.)* Was it a surprise, or was it predictable? Did the story end with the climax, or did it have a resolution?

Theme

Theme is an important idea that emerges from a story. Authors don't usually state the theme of a work outright, but let their readers decide for themselves which ideas are most important. For clues to theme, readers can look at the characters, the main events, and the conflicts in a story. You should also take a close look at what the characters learn, and how they change from the beginning of the story to the end. Most stories have several themes. At the conclusion of the novel, brainstorm some possible themes of *The Wind in the Willows*. The following diagram should help you get started.

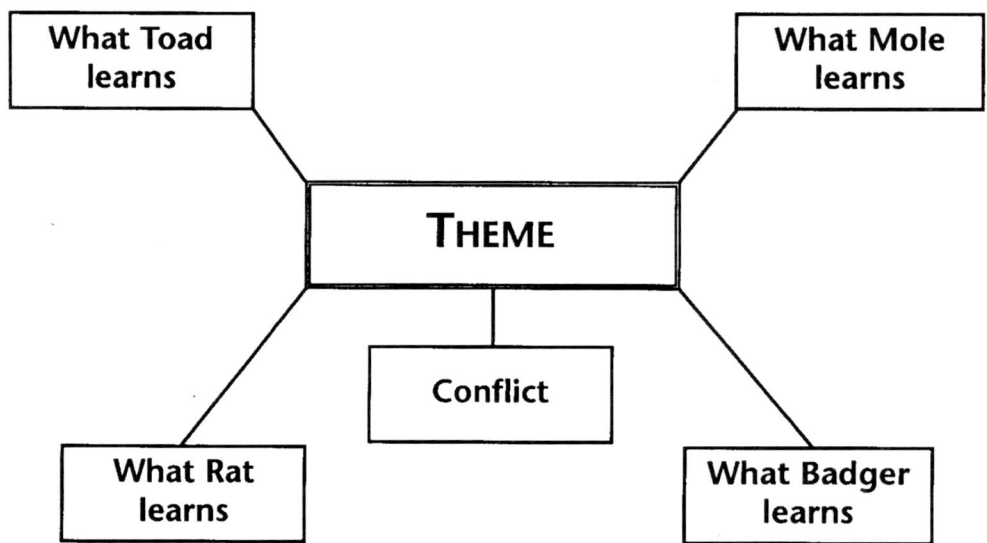

What issues did the author raise for you?

Some universal themes:

- Friendship
- Courage
- Survival
- Kindness
- Values

Using Predictions

We all make predictions as we read—little guesses about what will happen next, how a conflict will be resolved, which details will be important to the plot, which details will help fill in our sense of a character. Students should be encouraged to predict, to make sensible guesses as they read the novel.

As students work on their predictions, these discussion questions can be used to guide them: What are some of the ways to predict? What is the process of a sophisticated reader's thinking and predicting? What clues does an author give to help us make predictions? Why are some predictions more likely to be accurate than others?

Create a chart for recording predictions. This could be either an individual or class activity. As each subsequent chapter is discussed, students can review and correct their previous predictions about plot and characters as necessary.

Use the facts and ideas the author gives.

Use your own prior knowledge.

Apply any new information (i.e., from class discussion) that may cause you to change your mind.

Predictions
_____
_____
_____
_____
_____

Prediction Chart

What characters have we met so far?	What is the conflict in the story?	What are your predictions?	Why did you make those predictions?

Using Character Webs

Attribute webs are simply a visual representation of a character from the novel. They provide a systematic way for students to organize and recap the information they have about a particular character. Attribute webs may be used after reading the novel to recapitulate information about a particular character, or completed gradually as information unfolds. They may be completed individually or as a group project.

One type of character attribute web uses these divisions:

- How a character acts and feels. (How does the character act? How do you think the character feels? How would you feel if this happened to you?)

- How a character looks. (Close your eyes and picture the character. Describe him/her to me.)

- Where a character lives. (Where and when does the character live?)

- How others feel about the character. (How does another specific character feel about our character?)

In group discussion about the characters described in student attribute webs, the teacher can ask for backup proof from the novel. Inferential thinking can be included in the discussion.

Attribute webs need not be confined to characters. They may also be used to organize information about a concept, object, or place.

Attribute Web

The attribute web below will help you gather clues the author provides about a character in the novel. Fill in the blanks with words and phrases which tell how the character acts and looks, as well as what the character says and what others say about the character.

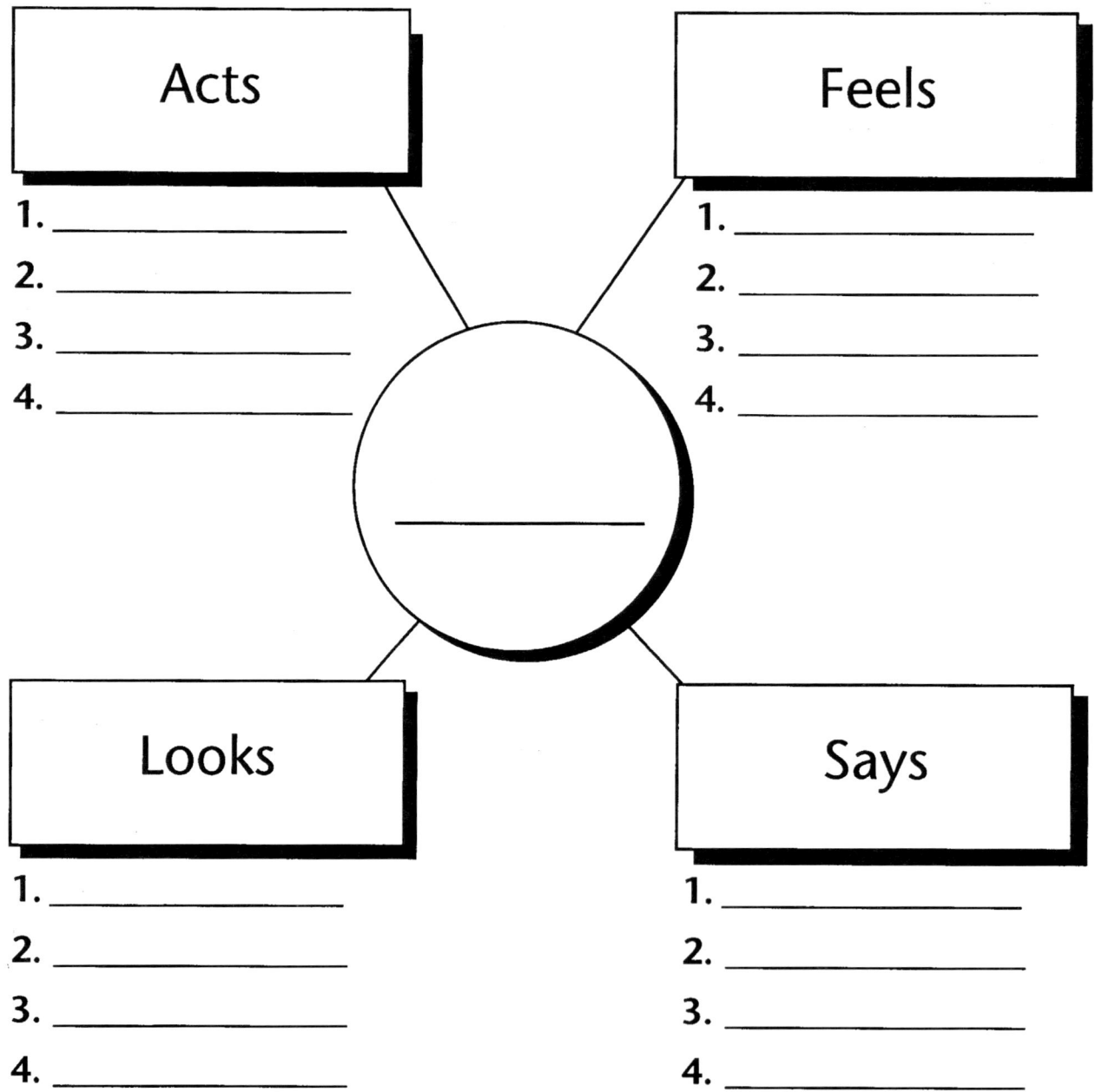

© Novel Units, Inc.   All rights reserved

Attribute Web

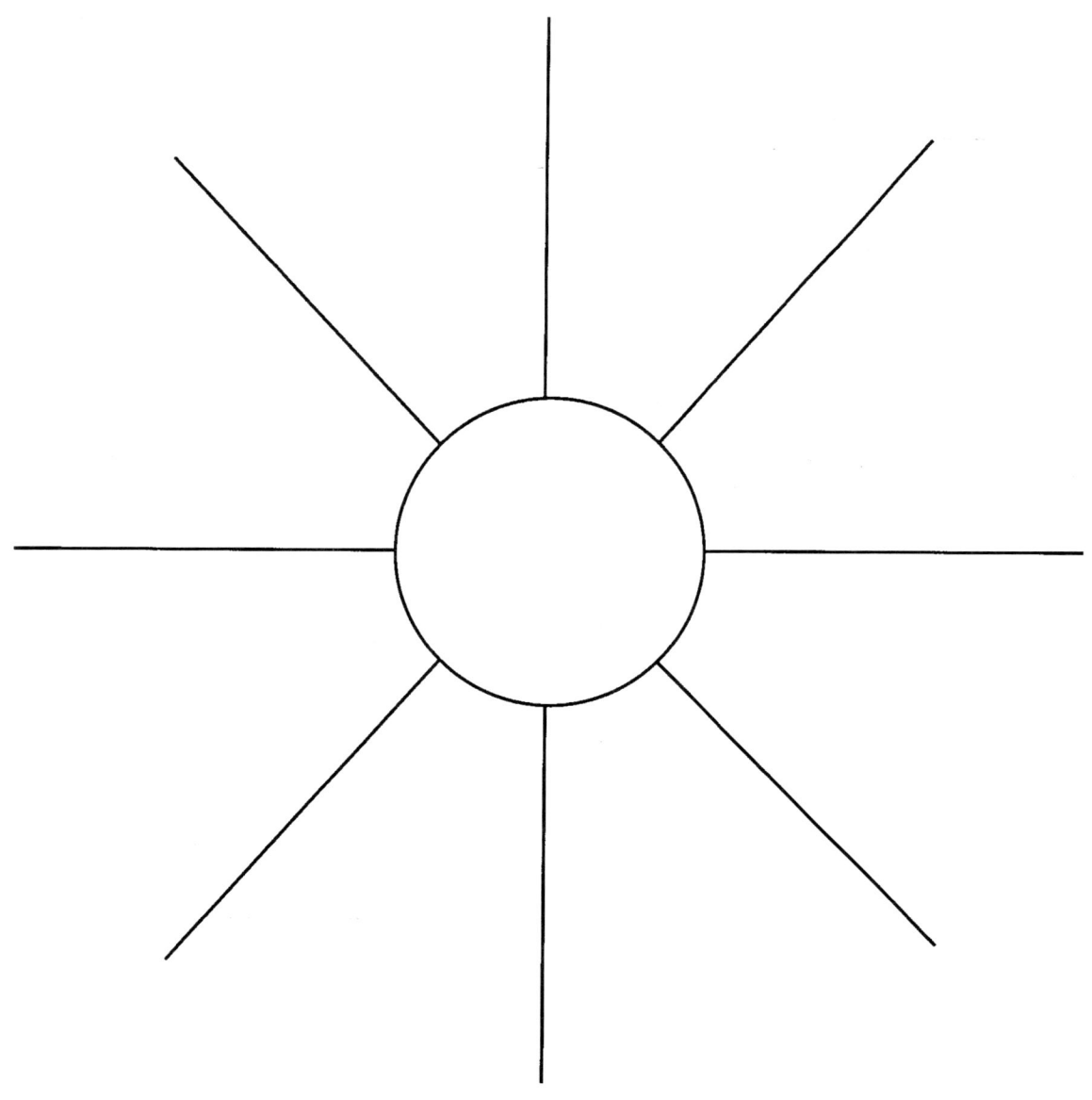

Story Map

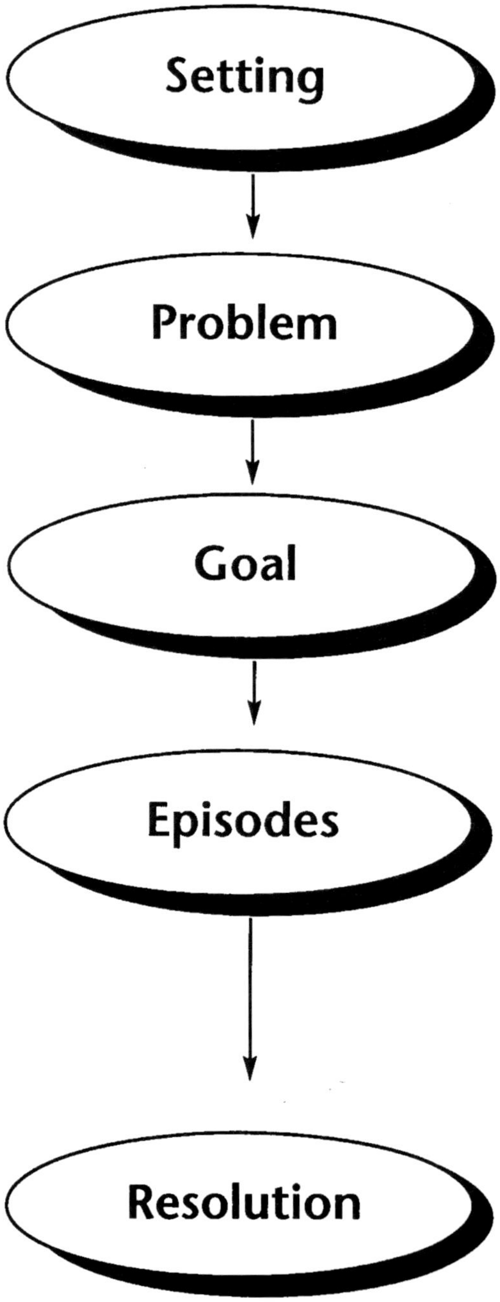

Setting

Characters _____
_____

Time and Place _____
_____

Problem

Problem _____
_____
_____

Goal

Goal _____
_____
_____

Episodes

Beginning ⟶ Development ⟶ Outcome
_____
_____
_____
_____
_____

Resolution

Resolution _____
_____
_____
_____

Chapter 1: "The River Bank"—Pages 1–18

Vocabulary

imperiously 1	seclusion 2	bowled 2	contemptuous 2
row 2	copses 2	meandered 3	sinuous 3
insatiable 3	bijou 3	pettishly 4	sculled 5
rapture 5	ecstasies 7	excursions 7	intoxicated 7
forbore 8	forbearance 9	trifle 9	stoats 9
etiquette 10	dwell 10	allude 10	weir 10
revelation 11	provender 12	impromptu 12	forthwith 12
wager-boat 12	togs 12	punting 13	reflectively 13
errant 13	athwart 13	affected 13	young bloods 13
forbade 14	prostrate 15	dismal 16	dejected 16
revived 17	sniggering 17	bedraggled 17	emancipated 18

Discussion Questions

1. What evidence can you give that this will be a realistic or unrealistic book of fiction? *(evidence for unrealistic fiction: a mole spring-cleaning his hole in the ground with brooms, dusters, ladders, and a pail of whitewash; a talking mole and other animals; a water rat who rows a boat and packs a picnic basket; etc.)*

2. Do you agree or disagree with Toad's thought that the "best part of a holiday is perhaps not so much to be resting yourself, as to see all the other fellows busy working" (page 3)? Why or why not?

3. How is Mole's experience by the river like that of a small child listening to a person tell stories? *(Answers will vary.)*

4. What did Rat do when he "sculled smartly across and made fast"? *(He rowed the boat quickly across the river and tied the boat to something on the other side.)*

5. Explain how and why you agree or disagree with Rat about messing about in boats. *(Answers will vary after students explain that, in Rat's opinion, there is nothing better than messing about, in, or with boats.)*

6. In what way was Mole drunk? *(He was not drunk on alcohol, but the excitement he was experiencing with all the new happenings in his life was causing him to feel drunk.)* Describe a time when you felt that kind of intoxication.

7. Describe someone you know whose feelings about his or her home area and the rest of the world are similar or dissimilar to those which Rat feels. *(Answers will vary, but must be based on the idea that Rat thinks his home offers everything he needs and the rest of the world isn't worth knowing about or exploring.)*

8. Explain what this sentence means in your own words: "An errant May-fly swerved unsteadily athwart the current in the intoxicated fashion affected by young bloods of May-flies seeing life." *(Answers will vary, for example, A May-fly that had strayed from the group or that was*

moving about aimlessly changed course and went across the current in an irregular fashion like young male May-flies that pretend a drunken swagger as they go about seeing life.)

9. When Mole was packing the basket after lunch, he found that it was not quite as pleasant as unpacking the basket had been, but he was determined to enjoy himself anyway (page 14). Explain how you or someone you know makes a not-so-pleasant task enjoyable. How could you make reading a chapter in a textbook or doing your homework enjoyable? *(Answers will vary.)*

10. Why did Mole get wet? *(He couldn't row very well, if at all, and overturned the boat. He let his jealousy of Rat's skill with the boat talk him into doing something foolish.)* Have you ever done something as foolish as what Mole did? What was it? What did you learn from that experience?

11. Was Rat's suggestion that Mole "trot up and down the towing-path as hard as he could" good advice or not? Why or why not? *(Yes, it was good advice because, as Mole trotted as hard as he could, his body would generate heat which would eventually dry his coat. Also, if Mole had been chilled by the water, the exercise would help to restore his body temperature.)*

Supplementary Activities

1. Prediction/Writing: Explain why you think Mole will or will not return to his home.

2. Science: Study life in and near a river. Collect some river water and look at it under a microscope. Make a model or a chart of river life.

3. Science: Study water safety. Bring a boating/swimming specialist into the class to talk about and demonstrate safe boating and swimming practices. Have the students role-play the safety practices.

Chapter 2: "The Open Road"—Pages 19–37

Vocabulary

acquaintance 21	affectionate 21	geniuses 21	conceited 21
dignified 22	mellowed 22	banqueting-hall 22	boisterously 23
squandered 24	trivialities 24	amiable 24	heath 24
common 24	hedgerows 24	downs 24	baccy 25
imploringly 25	fusty 25	wistfully 26	wavered 27
oblige 27	diplomatically 27	voluble 28	schemes 28
trudging 28	orchards 28	habitations 29	pathetically 29
exhausted 30	fatigues 30	consequence 30	momentous 31
overwhelming 31	precisely 31	brazen 31	morocco 31
passionate 31	utterly 32	heart-rendering 32	irredeemable 32
scoundrels 32	shoal 32	placid 32	despairingly 33
magnificent 34	hysterical 34	savagely 35	vouchsafed 35
exclusively 36	spell-bound 36		

Discussion Questions

1. Begin attribute webs for Rat and Mole. (See pages 13-15 of this guide.)

2. What did you learn about Mole in the five paragraphs after the song "Ducks' Ditty" on page 20? *(Mole is wishy-washy in his thoughts. He doesn't want to offend anyone so he will agree with whomever he is conversing, even if he has to contradict himself.)*

3. What does the italicized phrase in this sentence from page 24 mean? "I propose to devote the remainder of mine to it, and can only regret the wasted years, that lie behind me, *squandered in trivialities.*" *(The years were wasted on unimportant or ordinary things or activities.)*

4. What approach did Toad use to get Rat and Mole to accompany him on his trip? *(Toad could see that Mole was interested in the trip, even though he would abide by Rat's wishes not to go. Toad then changed tack and declared that the trip was for his friends' enjoyment rather than his. By emphasizing the joys of the trip to Mole—who was the easiest one to excite about the trip—he made Rat feel as though he was depriving his friend, Mole, of a glorious opportunity. As a result, Rat relented in order to make Mole happy. The meaning of the sentence, "He proceeded to play upon the inexperienced Mole as on a harp" should also be discussed in conjunction with this question.)* Describe a situation in which you used this same method to convince others to do something you wanted them to do.

Supplementary Activities

1. Prediction/Writing: What might happen now that Toad will soon have a car?

2. Compare/Contrast: How is Toad different from Rat and Mole? Use the following chart to organize this information.

Differences Among Toad, Rat, and Mole

CHARACTERISTICS	TOAD	RAT	MOLE
WORK ETHIC			
INTERESTS			
HOME			

3. Music: Have the students make up songs about an animal in the story or another animal they know very well. They could work individually or in small groups. Once the song has been written, they could perform it or record it for the class. Copies of the songs may be distributed to all the class members so they may also learn the songs.

Chapter 3: "The Wild Wood"—Pages 38–55

Vocabulary

solitary 39	loosestrife 40	luxuriant 40	gavotte 40
debonair 40	keen 40	undispersed 40	radiant 40
languorous 41	siesta 41	resolution 41	intimately 41
dells 41	quarries 41	masquerade 41	deceptions 41
exhilarating 42	quickset 42	caricatures 42	malice 43
anxiously 44	hearken 44	whither 45	vainly 45
verdant 45	goloshes 46	cudgel 46	valorous 46
forsaking 47	traverse 47	laboriously 47	guineas 48
faery 49	invincible 49	monotony 50	vary 50
hummocky 50	feeble 52	jig 52	obtuseness 52
sledge 53	exasperating 53	rodent 53	oblige 53
light-headed 53	astonished 54	hitherto 54	incredulous 54
penitence 54	majestic 54	theory 54	

Discussion Questions

1. Compare the students' predictions about whether Mole would ever go home with the additional information they have after reading Chapter 3.

2. How much time has passed since page 1? Have the students read orally the passages which support their answer. *(It started in early spring and is now winter. Some possible oral passages which could be read include: Page 1, "The Mole had been working very hard all morning, spring-cleaning his little home"; Page 2, "Jumping off all his four legs at once, in the joy of living and the delight of spring without its cleaning, he pursued his way across the meadow till he reached the hedge on the further side"; Page 39, "But the Badger never came along, and every day brought its amusements, and it was not till summer was long over, and cold and frost and miry ways kept them much indoors and the swollen river raced past outside their windows with a speed that mocked at boating of any sort or kind, that he found his thoughts dwelling again with much persistence on the solitary gray Badger, who lived his own life by himself, in his hole in the middle of the Wild Wood"; Page 39, "In the winter time the Rat slept a great deal, retiring early and rising late.")*

3. What do loosestrife, willow-herb, comfrey, dog-rose, and jerkin have in common? *(They are all flowers.)*

4. What new experiences did Mole have in this chapter? *(He experienced snow, the Wild Wood, and Mr. Badger.)*

5. What did Mole think was the terror of the Wild Wood? *(falling snow)*

6. Why do you think Rat prepared himself the way he did to find Mole? *(Answers will vary.)*

7. Give examples of the kind of communication problem Rat and Mole were having. *(In the example of the "doormat telling him something," Rat was talking about inferences he could make from the doormat being there while Mole was taking Rat literally and couldn't understand why Rat thought a doormat could talk at all. Other examples are possible.)*

Supplementary Activities

1. Prediction/Writing: Describe the kind of reception Mr. Badger will give Rat and Mole.

2. Attribute Webs: Add any new characteristics to the character attribute webs (pages 13-15 of this guide). Explain why you are adding each particular item.

Chapter 4: "Mr. Badger"—Pages 56-74

Vocabulary

down-at-heel 56	suspicious 56	exceedingly 56	perished 57
summons 58	paternally 58	apparent 58	draught 58
settles 58	mirth 59	sticking-plaster 59	repast 60
regrettable 60	strenuous 62	arduous 62	oppressive 63
accordance 63	injunctions 63	rashers 64	somnolence 65
monotonous 65	chivvying 66	famished 68	divert 68
staggered 70	ramifications 70	vaultings 70	masonry 70
obliterated 71	flourished 71	oppressing 72	confusedly 73
menacing 73	simultaneously 73	asperities 74	

Discussion Questions

1. Explain why you think Mr. Badger was or was not a good host. *(Good host: took their wet clothes, brought them dry clothes and slippers to put on, sat them near the fire, dressed Mole's cut on his shin, fed them well, didn't reprimand them for being out on such a night, listened to them, provided them with a place to sleep, took on an underground shortcut through the woods when they left. Poor host: left them to fix their own breakfast while he slept in the morning.)*

2. What did Mr. Badger and Mole have in common? *(They both were animals who normally live underground.)*

3. What did you think of the rabbit's response to Mole's problem? Under what circumstances have you or someone you've known responded to another person's need in the same way as the rabbit? *(Answers will vary.)*

4. How was Mr. Badger fortunate in his selection of his home site? *(The destruction of a previous city on the site had left tunnels and other openings underground that badger only had to clean out to make habitable for himself.)*

© Novel Units, Inc. All rights reserved

5. Explain what the statement "we must all live and let live" (page 72) means to Badger and to you. *(Answers will vary.)*

6. Based on what you know about Mole, will you keep or change your prediction about whether or not Mole will ever return to his home? *(Additional information in this chapter which might affect one's prediction: Page 63, Mole feels very comfortable underground; page 68, Badger extolls the virtues of living underground with which Mole agrees; page 74, Mole realizes he is "an animal of tilled field and hedgerow.")*

Supplementary Activities

1. Prediction/Writing: Explain why you do or do not think Badger, Rat, and Mole will be able to make Toad more sensible.

2. Social Studies: Study the rise and fall of various cities.

3. Science: Study the lives of animals that live underground, such as moles, badgers, chipmunks, ants, and some snakes. (You may want to add an ant farm to the classroom so the students can observe what happens underground.)

4. Pro/Con: Use the chart below to make a transparency, individual or group copies, or an enlarged wall chart to record the students' ideas on the advantages and disadvantages of living underground and above-ground.

Underground or Above-Ground?

	Advantages	Disadvantages
Underground		
Above-Ground		

Chapter 5: "Dulce Domum"—Pages 75–96

Vocabulary

tributary 75	dubiously 76	smouldering 78	pulsated 78
silhouetted 78	appurtenance 78	recognisable 78	filament 80
forsaken 80	captivating 80	reproachfully 80	plaintive 80
anguish 81	asunder 81	wafts 81	conjured 81
submissively 82	callous 82	paroxysm 82	sympathetically 83
recollection 83	anecdote 84	endeavoured 84	beguile 84
meagre 86	doleful 87	self-reproaches 87	roused 87
forage 88	dolorously 88	pâté de foie gras 88	expatiate 89
fallow 90	benison 91	anon 91	clangorous 92
chilblains 93	Barbary corsair 93	rancour 95	

Discussion Questions

1. How did Rat and Mole feel when they looked in the windows of the houses in the village? *(They felt wistful, anxious to be home, etc.)*

2. What was the summons that Mole received? *(He received a sense that home was nearby.)* Have you ever felt that you were close to something you have known before? If so, what was it and when did it happen?

3. Why did Rat turn around and go back to look for Mole's home? *(because he felt sorry for Mole; because he wanted to relieve Mole's grief about not visiting his old home)*

4. Describe Mole's home. *(Refer to pages 86-89.)*

5. Explain the following statement: "He must needs go and caress his possessions and take a lamp and show off their points to his visitor and expatiate on them" (page 89). *(Mole needed to touch the things in his home and take Rat for a tour of his home as he talked at length about the special characteristics of each piece.)*

6. Compare the abilities of Mole and Rat to provide for unexpected guests. *(Mole seemed unable to cope, not only with providing food, but also with carrying on a conversation with the field mice. Once the food was taken care of, Mole relaxed and was able to converse. Rat was very resourceful in that he sent someone for supplies, utilized some of what was available in Mole's home, and delegated the various jobs of preparation when the supplies arrived.)*

7. How did Rat cheer up Mole? *(Rat cheered up Mole by returning to look for Mole's home, praising the special qualities of Mole's home, handling situations which were overwhelming to Mole, etc.)*

8. What did Mole finally realize? *(He realized that his home was very plain and simple, yet very special to him. He also realized that he didn't want to give up the opportunity to continue experiencing new places, animals, and things in the above-ground world. Knowing that he could come home provided comfort to him.)*

Supplementary Activities
1. Prediction/Writing: What do you think will happen next?

2. Music: Sing some English carols and/or have the students make up a carol in small groups about what they do during the winter holidays.

Chapter 6: "Mr. Toad"—Pages 97–115

Vocabulary

wonted 97	arraying 98	habiliments 98	ere 99
gaiters 99	gauntleted 99	panoply 100	contemptuously 101
discourse 101	dubiously 102	sullenly 102	scandalized 102
eloquent 102	repentant 103	emphatically 103	persuasion 103
uncouth 104	languid 104	artfullest 105	nuisance 106
improvised 108	mullion 108	caustic 108	duffer 108
crestfallen 108	turbid 109	merits 110	sonorous 112
incorrigible 112	rogue 112	ruffian 112	cowering 112
impertinence 112	cheeking 113	portcullis 114	abhorrence 114
casquet 114	corselet 114	vizards 114	warders 114
halberds 114	gaoler 114	murrain 114	

Discussion Questions

1. Explain why you would or would not like to have your plans disrupted as Badger did to Mole and Rat. *(Answers will vary, but they should be based on the way Badger disrupted Mole and Rat's plans for the day on short notice.)*

2. Explain how you think Toad felt when Badger, Rat, and Mole took charge of him. *(Answers will vary.)*

3. Give examples from your own life when the clothes you had on made a difference in the way you acted. *(Answers will vary.)*

4. Describe how someone you have known acted like Toad. *(Comparisons to Toad's actions should be included. A listing of those actions can be found on pages 100-101.)* Did anyone ever try to change him/her and, if so, how did they go about it? What was the result?

5. Who do you think knew Toad best—Badger, Rat, or Mole? Why? *(Answers will vary.)*

6. Explain why you think the brain did or did not triumph over brute force in this chapter. *(Answers will vary.)*

Supplementary Activities

1. Prediction/Writing: What do you think will happen to Toad now?

2. Compare/Contrast: Compare the punishments for Toad's crimes with punishments for similar crimes in our society today. The following chart may be used for this purpose. Some research

may need to be done by the students before this can be completed.

Punishment for Crimes

Crime	Toad's Time	Today
Stealing a car		
Reckless driving		
Gross impertinence to an officer		

3. Attribute Webs: Begin attribute webs for Badger and Toad. Add to Rat and Mole's webs if possible.

Chapter 7: "The Piper at the Gates of Dawn"—Pages 116–131

Vocabulary

selvedge 116	articulate 120	phosphorescence 120	raiment 120
bulrushes 121	oisiers 121	rapt 121	dandled 122
transfixed 122	unsurpassable 122	tumultuous 123	Awe 125
smote 125	august 125	Presence 125	dominant 125
imminent 125	sward 126	podgy 126	unutterable 126
capricious 126	oblivion 127	demigod 127	haunting 127
jaunt 128	lustily 128	restraint 128	vigil 129
ford 129	amble 129	hark 130	lilting 130
frolic 130	fret 130	rent 130	waifs 130

Discussion Questions

1. What is the effect on parents when children run away? Was it any different for the Otters? *(no)*

2. Why were the Otters more worried this time? *(Page 117, He had been missing for several days; no trace of him had been found; none of the other animals had seen him; Portly hadn't learned how to swim very well yet; the presence of the weir; the high water level; and traps.)*

3. Why do you think Rat heard the music before Mole did? *(Answers will vary.)*

4. Why were "Him," "Awe," "Presence," "Friend," and "Helper" all capitalized on page 125? *(They were capitalized because they represented a god.)*

5. Explain why the Rat was both afraid and unafraid of seeing the demigod. *(Answers will vary.)*

6. Why do you think the demigod appeared to Rat and Mole and not to the parents who had also been looking for the baby otter? *(Some clues may be found in the last song Rat heard, on page 130.)*

7. Why would the demigod cause them to forget everything they had seen and heard? *(He caused them to forget so they could still enjoy earthly pleasures.)*

Supplementary Activities

1. Writing/Drama: While working in groups, have the students create their own story about Pan or a god of their own making. Have the students share their stories orally, dramatically, or in book form.

2. Music: Play recorded music performed on the pan-pipes. Ask the students about their reactions to it. Have them compare this form of music to what they listen to daily.

3. Science: Have the students create a model of a river with a weir, a ford, and other features characteristic of a river.

4. Literature: Locate other books with stories about Pan, the Greek god of pastures, flocks, and shepherds, as well as other books about Greek gods and goddesses. Read one or two orally, or have the students read them silently.

Chapter 8: "Toad's Adventures"—Pages 132–151

Vocabulary

disporting 132	audacious 132	lurid 132	bestowed 132
languish 132	lamentations 133	shrouded 133	antimacasser 133
piebald 133	fender 135	avidity 136	sanguine 136
affably 137	stipulation 139	artifice 139	untarnished 139
quaking 140	sallies 140	exploit 141	shunted 141
humiliating 141	repartees 141	uncanny 142	stringency 142
obstructing 144	baffled 145	baulked 145	pettifogging 145
reviled 145	rapture 146	astonishment 147	frivolous 147
truncheons 148	supplication 148	proprietor 148	embankment 150
motley 150	sarcastic 151		

Discussion Questions

1. Explain why you think the jailer's (gaoler's) daughter was either good or bad for Toad. *(The answers will be open-ended, but should reflect knowledge of what happened between the girl and Toad.)*

2. Do you think the girl and her aunt were trying to trick Toad when the girl asked him to take off his coat and waistcoat before putting on the dress? Why or why not? *(Answers will vary.)*

3. Could a toad dress in a washerwoman's clothes to disguise himself in real life? Why or why not? *(Answers will vary.)*

4. What internal conflict did Toad experience as he walked out of the prison? *(Pages 140-141, The internal conflict he experienced pertained to making the expected off-color responses to the persons he encountered, while still not going over the boundaries of good taste, so he could maintain his dignity.)*

5. Why do you think the ticket clerk didn't believe Toad? *(One answer might be that Toad wasn't dressed as though he was a person who could pay. Other answers are possible.)*

6. Explain why you think the engine-driver made a good, or not-so-good, trade. *(Answers will vary, but should refer to washing a few shirts for him to ride on the train.)*

7. What fault of Toad's began to make the engine-driver suspicious? *(Toad talked too much. In this case, he sang too much.)*

8. Compare what the engine-driver did for Toad, after Toad made his confession, with what you think most engine-drivers would do in the same situation. *(As a point of comparison, the facts on pages 149-150 should be included.)*

9. Orally read what the fox said to Toad on page 151 in the way you think he would have said it. *(It should be read in a sarcastic way.)*

Supplementary Activity
Prediction/Writing: What do you think will happen to Toad tomorrow?

Chapter 9: "Wayfarers All"—Pages 152–174

Vocabulary

rowans 152	premonitions 152	quiver 153	pinions 153
peremptory 153	table-d'hôte 153	en pension 153	self-sufficing 153
reminiscence 158	fascinated 158	abandonment 159	treachery 159
tawny 159	pulsate 160	panorama 160	saluted 160
gesture 160	courtesy 160	reapers 161	Constantinople 162
quays 163	foreshores 163	gallant 163	circumscribed 164
epitome 164	hoisted 164	cistern 164	Adriatic 164
gondolas 164	enthralled 165	phantom 165	vaporous 165
prejudiced 165	lay to 166	hove 166	Marseilles 166
inadvertently 167	hatches 167	commendations 167	assuaged 167
heraldings 168	league 168	vibrant 168	vintage 168
compelled 168	North-Easter 169	mandoline 169	caique 169
plaintive 169	leech 169	gallant 169	lagoons 169
perils 169	stanchions 170	tarry 170	bide 170
irrevocable 171	blithesome 171	mechanically 171	satchel 171
deliberation 171	resolutely 172	dogged 172	fixity 172

grappling 172	desperately 172	collapsed 172	hysterical 172
seizure 172	unenlightened 172	listless 173	dejected 173
gratification 173	inevitable 173	ricks 173	sheaves 173
distilling 174	cordials 174	lyrical 174	

Discussion Questions

1. Do you think the analogy in paragraph one on page 153 is accurate? Why or why not? *(Answers will vary.)*

2. What was the indirect message the field-mouse tried to express to Rat on page 155? *(He was trying to tell Rat to be more careful and look where he was going so he wouldn't hurt himself and make undignified remarks.)*

3. Why do you think the swallows and Rat had different opinions about the swallows' pending trip south? *(Answers will vary, but might include references to the animals' life patterns.)*

4. Were the swallows ever able to change Rat's opinion? If so, how did they do it and what was the result? *(Yes, the swallows were able to ignite in Rat the same desire to head south, but only for a brief time. More than likely the swallows were unaware of Rat's capitulation—because it occurred only in Rat's thoughts.)*

5. What do you think is the significance of the visitor rat saying that he was, "following the old call, back to the old life, the life which is mine and will not let me go"? *(Page 162, Literally, he could mean that he was going back to the life in the country that he had before he set out on his travels, but by saying "the life which is mine and will not let me go," he may have been referring to his destiny. For each animal on earth, there is a natural life pattern. The visitor rat had deviated from that pattern, that destiny, and was now being called back to it.)*

6. On the map of Europe, locate the places the visitor rat had been and chart his travels. *(to Constantinople, to the Grecian Islands, to Levant, to the coast of Adriatic, to Venice, down the Italian shore to Palermo, to Sardinia and Corsica, to Alassio, to Marseilles, from port to port of Spain, to Lisbon, Oporto, and Bordeaux, to Cornwall and Devon, up the Channel to a port in England, then inland, then southwestwards to a sea town that clings along one steep side of the harbor)*

7. Explain what the phrase "allowanced as to water" means. *(page 163, rationed water)*

8. How did Mole cure Rat? How long did it take? *(He wrestled Rat to the ground, took him home, locked the door, locked his suitcase up, waited for Rat's hysterical seizure to pass, listened to Rat attempt to explain, told Rat of events that were happening around them at the time, gave Rat a pencil and paper, and suggested that it had been a long time since Rat had written any poetry; The process took from fall to midwinter.)*

9. Explain why you think Mole was or was not a good friend to Rat. *(Answers will vary.)*

Supplementary Activities

1. Writing: Compare and contrast the characteristics of someone who is a good friend versus someone who is not a true friend.

2. Social Studies: Have each students or group of students research one of the places to which the visitor rat traveled, and then prepare a project and present what they have learned to the rest of the class.

3. Geography: Challenge the students to figure out which sea town was the one to which the visitor rat traveled southwestwards.

Chapter 10: "The Further Adventures of Toad"—Pages 175–199

Vocabulary

beseeching 175	pursuit 176	triumphal 176	toilet 176
dispelled 176	threaded 176	taut 177	brawny 177
tiller 177	abreast 177	post-haste 178	humble 178
acknowledgements 178	gentry 179	idle 179	trollops 179
shirking 180	deprive 181	recollect 181	unrestrainedly 182
viciously 182	relinquished 182	impeded 183	indignation 183
mangle 183	abandoning 184	gesticulating 184	caravan 185
voluptuous 185	solace 185	trifling 185	qualm 185
disposed 186	Oxford 190	revive 193	proposal 194
prudent 195	submerged 196	encumbered 196	floundering 196
ecstasies 196	unscathed 197	grudging 197	excursionists 197
ingenious 197	ceasing 198	triumphant 198	contend 198

Discussion Questions

1. Describe the experience Toad had washing the clothes. *(Nothing Toad did seemed to make the clothes any cleaner and he became very frustrated.)*

2. Describe the sequence of events that led to Toad being thrown from the barge and explain why Toad was finally thrown from the barge. *(Toad lied about himself and his occupation. He was trapped into either telling the truth or washing the clothes. He got madder and madder as he washed the clothes. The washerwoman laughed at him. Toad lost his temper, called the washerwoman names, revealed his true identity, and bragged about himself. It seemed that the washerwoman threw him from the barge more because he was a dirty old toad than because he called her names.)*

3. How did Toad get revenge on the washerwoman? Was Toad justified in getting revenge on her? Why or why not? *(Toad stole the washerwoman's horse so she had no way to pull the barge. Answers will vary for the other questions.)*

4. Describe a time when you wanted to get revenge on someone. What else could you have done instead? *(Answers will vary.)*

5. What did you think of the bargain Toad struck for the horse, and why? *(Answers will vary, but should make reference to the six shillings and sixpence plus the breakfast that he got for the horse.)* Students could calculate how much, in dollars, the bargain would be worth (at today's rate and the rate it would have been when the book was written).

6. How did Toad's pride and conceit cause him problems? *(He became overconfident and careless. Specific examples may also be given.)*

7. How did a mistaken identity help Toad? *(It helped him get a ride on the motor-car and an opportunity to drive it. Students may also cite earlier examples of how a mistaken identity helped Toad.)*

8. What emotions did Toad experience in this chapter? *(wonder 175, happiness 176, excitement 176, confidence 176, annoyance 176, friendliness 178, humility 178, nervousness 179, frightened 181, resigned 181, desperate 181, cross 181, dismay 182, frustrated 182, vicious 182, furious 182, indignant 183, revenge 183, contented 184, satisfied 184, clever 184, desire 184, surprised 186, satiated 188, affectionate 188, careless 188, self-confident 192, frightened 192, despair 192, miserable 192, eager 195, prudent 195, annoyed 195, fearless 195, wonder 196, fear 196, ecstasy 196, clever 196, dismay 196, desperate 196, exhaustion 197, relieved 198)*

Supplementary Activity
Writing: Explain why you think pride and conceit are or are not desirable characteristics to have. Give examples to support your position.

Chapter 11: " 'Like Summer Tempests Came His Tears' "—Pages 200–224

Vocabulary

hoist 200	evasions 200	nobly 200	disguises 200
subterfuges 200	humbugged 200	bedraggled 201	disreputable 201
apparently 201	rakishly 201	contemplating 201	cunning 202
ignominiously 202	jawed 203	mutinously 203	suppressed 203
infamously 205	smirk 205	simultaneously 206	desperate 206
skirmishing 206	conservatory 206	villains 206	grub 206
vulgar 206	magistrates 208	palings 208	prudently 208
crestfallen 208	tranquil 209	parapet 209	indignant 209
trying 210	submissive 210	appeased 210	reproachfully 211
scheming 211	contriving 211	privations 211	touzled 212
portentous 212	despondent 212	victuals 212	liberally 213
contrition 215	severity 216	worthy 216	volatile 216
salon 217	sarcasm 223	accoutrement 223	

Discussion Questions
1. Who do you think assessed Toad more accurately, and why? *(Answers will vary.)*

2. Explain what the sentence, "And all because you must needs go and steal a motor-car" on page 202, means. *(It means "had to go.")*

3. On page 205, Rat tells Toad that the animals took sides regarding Toad's experiences stealing the automobile. Would you side with the River-bankers or the Wild Wood animals regarding Toad? Why? *(Answers will vary.)*

4. Explain why you would or would not like to have a friend like Toad. *(Answers will vary.)*

5. Have you ever known anyone like Toad? If so, describe what he or she did that was like Toad. How did people try to help that person, and were they successful? *(Answers will vary.)*

6. How did Mole undo all that Rat and Badger had tried to reinforce with Toad? *(He came in exuberantly to see Toad and praised his cleverness, ingeniousness, and intelligence. This approach played to Toad's conceit and derring-do rather than to being more sensible.)*

7. Do you know people like Toad who can't keep secrets? How did it make you feel when you told someone you trusted a secret and he or she told it anyway? What did you do the next time you wanted to tell a secret? *(Answers will vary.)*

8. What difference do you think Badger attached to the terms "teach 'em" versus "learn 'em" when he said, "'But we don't *want* to teach 'em,' replied the Badger. 'We want to *learn* 'em—learn 'em, learn 'em! And what's more, we're going to *do* it, too!'" (page 220)? *(Answers will vary.)*

9. Explain why Mole's actions were so clever. *(He tricked and antagonized the stoats. He told them a lie about what was going to happen in order to scare them and make them easily frightened off when the real attack came. That way, they would run instead of staying to defend their positions.)*

Supplementary Activity
Prediction/Writing: Explain whether you think Toad's friends will ever eventually abandon him and why they will or won't do it.

Chapter 12: "The Return of Ulysses"—Pages 225–244

Vocabulary
truncheon 225	pacified 227	groped 227	carousing 228
wrathfully 230	emitting 230	debris 231	consummate 234
unction 241	delicacies 243	mottled 243	fractious 244

Discussion Questions
1. Were Badger's suspicions about Toad's intentions correct? Why or why not? *(Yes; he suspected Toad of not following through on the invitations in a proper manner and was proven correct when he intercepted the weasel on his way to deliver the invitations.)*

2. Explain in what ways Toad's behavior at the banquet was either expected or unexpected. *(Answers will vary.)*

3. Why do you think the Wild Wood was no longer a fearful place for Rat, Toad, and Mole? *(Answers will vary.)*

4. What did the weasel children think of Rat, Toad, Mole, and Badger? *(The weasel children looked up to Rat, Toad, and Mole, but they feared Badger unjustly.)*

5. Give examples from other stories or movies where parents told their children that they should be good for fear of what some person or character would do to them if they weren't good. Is this a good technique for parents to use? Why or why not? *(Answers will vary.)*

Supplementary Activity

Prediction/Writing: Using a Venn diagram like the one below, have the students note the similarities and differences between the four heroes of this story with any current group of heroes in TV cartoons or comics.

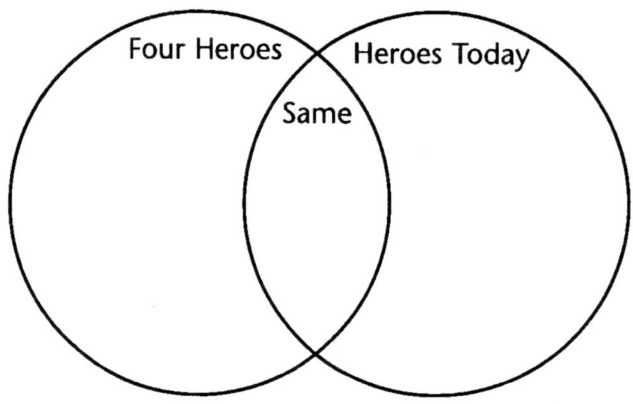

Culminating Activities

1. How does this story compare with other animal stories you have read?

2. Summarize the story using the story diagram below. What purpose is there in a story diagram? How would using a story map help an author?

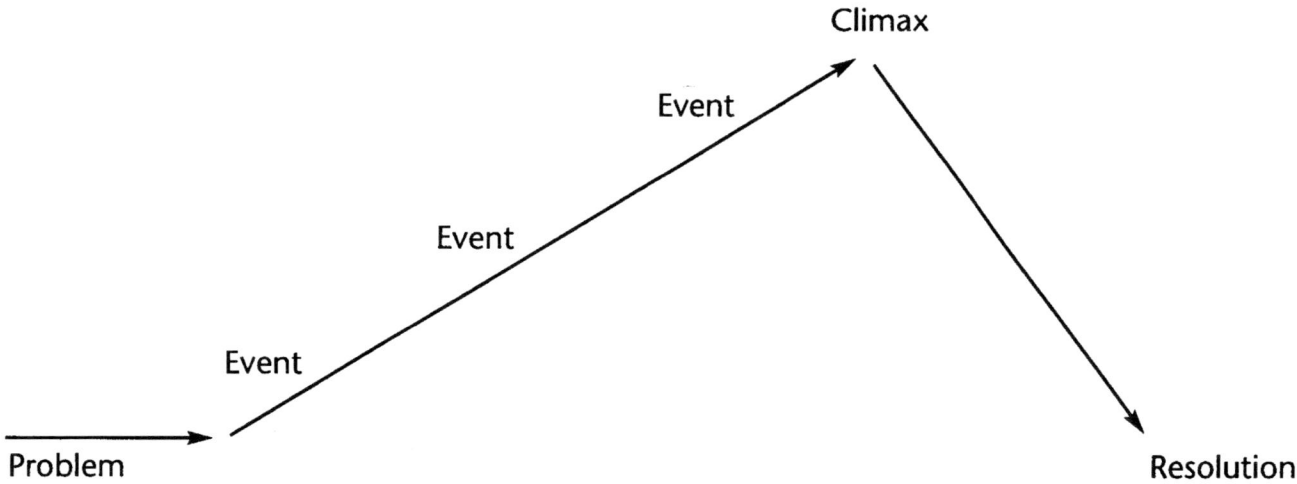

3. Characterization: Characters are developed by what they say, think, and do, as well as how others in the novel react to them. What did you learn about Mole, Toad, Rat, and Badger? Review your attribute webs. Which characters in this novel provide wisdom and perspective? Which character in the story is most like you? How do the characters change during the story? If you could be one of the characters in the story, who would you choose to be? Do any of the characters in the book remind you of people you know, or characters from other stories?

4. Setting: Where does the story take place? What parts of the setting could be real? How important is the setting to the story? How do the various settings contribute to the mood and move the plot along? If you were making a movie based on *The Wind in the Willows*, where would you film your movie?

5. Theme is the novel's central idea. What is the author's message? Why do you think the author wrote this story? What do you think is the most important thing to remember about this story? Support your ideas for the theme(s) by using examples from the novel. What does Toad learn?

6. Which parts of this story were most vivid and interesting to you? Which parts made you laugh?

Post-reading Extension Activities

Writing Activities
1. Write a diary entry that one of the characters in *The Wind in the Willows* might write.

2. Pick one of the main characters in the novel and write five questions that you would like to ask in order to understand why the character acted that way.

3. Add another chapter to the novel (involving the same characters) that would make the story more exciting.

4. An epilogue is an addition to a story that tells what happened later. Choose a time in the future, and write a brief epilogue to the activities of Mole, Toad, Rat, and Badger.

Listening and Speaking Activities
1. Stage a TV interview with some of the characters in the story. For homework, students playing each role gather impressions about what their character is like. Other students make lists of interview questions.

2. Retell an episode from your favorite chapter from the viewpoint of a different character.

3. Work with a partner to create an imaginary dialogue between yourself and one of the characters in the novel. The character you choose should act and respond in the same manner as in the book. With your partner, present your dialogue to the class.

Art Activities
1. Secure a sheet of mural paper at least 24 feet long, which has been marked off into two-foot sections, to a wall or clear place on the floor. Divide the class into twelve small groups and let each group draw a chapter number from a hat. Each group must plan and complete a drawing which depicts the most important event of that chapter.

2. Draw a picture of the four friends—Rat, Mole, Toad, and Badger.

3. Make a collage on a large piece of posterboard. Divide the posterboard into sections. Each section should represent a character from the novel. Use magazine cut-outs or drawings of your own.

Music and Writing Activity
Divide the class into twelve groups. Each group writes a verse to a song retelling the story of *The Wind in the Willows*. Copy the verses and have the groups practice singing them. Hand or body gestures may be added. Volunteer to sing the song to other classes, the whole school, or assembled parents.

Assessment for *The Wind in the Willows*

Assessment is an ongoing process. The following ten items can be completed during the novel study. Once finished, the student and teacher will check the work. Points may be added to indicate the level of understanding.

Name _____ Date _____

Student   **Teacher**

_____   _____   1. As you read, keep a response log.

_____   _____   2. Compare Toad with one of his friends using a Venn diagram.

_____   _____   3. Complete five vocabulary activities.

_____   _____   4. Write another adventure for Toad.

_____   _____   5. Change three things in the novel and explain how these changes would make a difference. Make a list of these changes and compare with your classmates.

_____   _____   6. Study life in (and near) a river. Collect some river water and look at it under a microscope. Make a model or chart of river life.

_____   _____   7. Complete the chart on the differences among Toad, Rat, and Mole. (See page 19 of this guide.)

_____   _____   8. Compare and contrast the characteristics of someone who is a good friend versus someone who is not a true friend.

_____   _____   9. Write a diary entry for one of the characters in the novel.

_____   _____   10. Write a self-evaluation about your study of this novel.

Notes